Daily Self-Care Journal for Black Women

A 365-Day Guided Journal for Self-Discovery. The Perfect Tool to Help Black Women Build Own Awareness, Stronger Habits, and Life Foundations

TAMICA JONES

Table of Contents

Introduction

The extremely pivotal, yet the most neglected aspect of a happy existence is self-care. The most underrated of all habits, it has the potential to redefine your way of life. It can help simplify and trace your path to success. It will aid you in achieving your goals, in eliminating stress and anxiety from your life, and in taking positive strides toward your larger purpose on a daily basis. You will no longer have to fret about unfulfilled tasks, or feel insignificant or inadequate in the chaotic race of existence. Discovering personal strengths and weaknesses, building healthy habits, and laying the foundation for a wholesome lifestyle, are some of the consequences of maintaining a self-care regime.

The practice of nurturing oneself can be grouped under the following categories.

Physical self-care: This means taking active steps to ensure that your physical fitness is in its best shape. This may take the form of inculcating healthy habits, like exercising for 30 minutes every day, or making positive changes like attempting to reduce your daily or weekly alcohol intake.

Mental self-care: As can be implied from the title, this facet of caring for yourself involves maintaining a productive intellectual, emotional, and creative state of mind at all times. Getting close to nature, finding ways to manage your anxiety, and identifying the stress reduction approach that works for you, are all positive steps toward achieving a healthy mind.

Social self-care: Humans are beings that thrive on mutual interactions. Making the effort to build strong personal relationships is crucial to self-acceptance and self-love. Embarking on family holidays, planning outings with friends, and participating in community activities are some of the useful practices in this aspect.

Spiritual self-care: Contrary to popular belief, this facet of self-care does not necessarily mean becoming more religious. Instead, it signifies the identification and acknowledgment of the presence of a higher power within your existence. This can be achieved by either reading holy scriptures, or by practicing self-actualisation techniques like meditation regularly.

A highly effective approach to stimulate positive growth in every dimension of self-care is to incorporate journalling into your everyday routine. Writing down your strengths, weaknesses, goals, successes, setbacks, fears, apprehensions, and experiences is the only way to free yourself from the bondage of judgment and discover the best version of yourself. Through the succeeding pages of this publication, you will find the median to not only work toward becoming more self-assured, but you will also be able to evaluate your progress in your journey toward self-understanding, self-improvement, self-acceptance, and self-love.

Chapter 1: Principles of Self-Care

In order to integrate self-care habits into your routine seamlessly, it is important to keep in mind the principles that are central to the concept. The primary ones among these are discussed below.

Conscious Integration

While including self-care practices into your everyday regime, it is important to incorporate them as valuable elements of your routine, and not as additions to your long list of daily obligations. For instance, while attempting to spend time close to nature, instead of adding the same to your to-do list as a separate task, you could choose to walk to your workplace, or spend your leisure hours by the riverside.

Mindful Choices

While picking the self-care activities to be seamlessly merged into your everyday routine, it is crucial to select those tasks that accelerate your progress toward your larger objective. In other words, it is important to set self-care goals that aid personal and professional growth. For example, while binge watching Netflix at home may be a relaxing break from the stresses of everyday life, choosing the option to read a book instead is a value-adding, self-care change.

Personal Freedom

As the pressures of everyday existence increase, the first element of a happy life that is neglected is self-care. It is sometimes overlooked to the extent that many begin to label it as a sign of self-obsession or selfishness. To truly benefit from the innumerable advantages of self-care, it is important to embrace the concept without any traces of guilt. It is vital to reiterate to yourself that in order to be able to radiate confidence, love, and care, it is first important to understand and accept yourself. Therefore, caring for yourself is not a healthy choice that you must make, but rather it is an indispensable necessity that should be a way of life.

Observe and React

While making self-care inclusions into your routine, it is crucial to acknowledge and understand your body's responses to them. Since human beings are diverse creatures, the same self-care practices can evoke ironic sentiments in two different individuals. For example, meditating for a few minutes may lead to mental peace in one person, while visiting a therapist might be necessary for another to experience the same feeling. Therefore, it is crucial to select those self-care practices that improve your physical, mental, social, and spiritual state of being. Equally important is to evaluate the sense of satisfaction that you feel after each activity, and to adjust the same as required so as to reap maximum benefits from the rewarding art of self-care.

Daily Self-Care Practices

Below is a list of self-care activities that you may consider including in your routine. It is however, important that you modify or substitute these suggestions based on your physical, mental, social, and spiritual limitations.

- Exercise for at least 20 minutes every day.

- Play a sport of your choice.

- Consume a diet free of white sugar and processed food for a day.

- Attempt a short run on the street every morning.

- Cultivate a new hobby.

- Journal every day.

- Read a book that is unrelated to your work.

- Talk to a friend or a family member outside of your household.

- Spend time with people of different age groups.

- Do a simple act of goodness, like assisting a disabled person on the street.

- Meditate for at least 5 minutes.

- Visit a place of worship of your preferred faith, or attend a community event.

- Water your plants, walk your dog, or simply take up a DIY task.

Chapter 2: Self-Care Tips

While creating a self-care regime it will help to keep the following additional points in mind.

Physical Self-Care

1. It is important to define your physical goals and to attempt tasks that help you take positive steps toward their accomplishment. Building overall fitness, increasing your immunity, weight loss/weight gain, reducing the symptoms of existing medical conditions, achieving a healthy skin, getting adequate rest, etc., are examples of physical targets.

2. To sustain self-care over a period of time, it is vital to choose activities that you enjoy. Do not feel compelled to play soccer if you prefer a hike instead.

3. Give yourself what your body needs on a given day. If you are sleep deprived, set a self-care goal to satisfy that deficiency.

Mental Self-Care

1. Do not be bound by societal stereotypes. If visiting a therapist improves your mental health, set it as a priority task on your self-care list.

2. It is vital to be open to experimentation when it comes to mental self-care activities. You will never realize the healing power of a warm soothing bath until you try it.

3. Consistency and persistence is paramount to mental self-care. If you start with meditation for instance, practice it for a considerable period of time regularly to reap its benefits.

Spiritual Self-Care

1. Keep an open mind and wholeheartedly embrace the spiritual changes that you make for your own well-being.

2. Change spiritual self-care practices frequently to avoid boredom or premature withdrawal.

3. Believe in the power of your mind.

References

Chu, L. (2010, July 20). *5 principles of self-care for health professionals*. KevinMD. https://www.kevinmd.com/2010/07/5-principles-selfcare-health-professionals.html

Planned Parenthood. (n.d.). *Six types of self-care*. Secure Everyaction. https://secure.everyaction.com/p/Pg5bqblugE6-NGId09RIcQ2

(S) (M) (T) (W) (T) (F) (S) /   /

⭐ Today I'm grateful for ...

🏔 My goal: What are you looking toward?

🎯 Today Targets: 30 Min. Time Blocks:

🌟 What will make today great?

Plan to reality score: _ _ _ _ _ _ /10

Progress towards goal

- [ ] last week
- [ ] this week
- [ ] remaining

"dreams DON'T WORK UNLESS you do"

(S) (M) (T) (W) (T) (F) (S)   /   /

⭐ Today I'm grateful for ...

- - - - - - - - - - - - - - - - - - - -
- - - - - - - - - - - - - - - - - - - -
- - - - - - - - - - - - - - - - - - - -
- - - - - - - - - - - - - - - - - - - -

🚩 My goal: What are you looking toward?

- - - - - - - - - - - - - - - - - - - -
- - - - - - - - - - - - - - - - - - - -
- - - - - - - - - - - - - - - - - - - -

🎯 Today Targets: 30 Min. Time Blocks:

_____

- - - - - - - - - - - - - - - - - - - -
- - - - - - - - - - - - - - - - - - - -
- - - - - - - - - - - - - - - - - - - -

_____

- - - - - - - - - - - - - - - - - - - -
- - - - - - - - - - - - - - - - - - - -

_____

- - - - - - - - - - - - - - - - - - - -
- - - - - - - - - - - - - - - - - - - -

🌟 What will make today great?

- - - - - - - - - - - - - - - - - - - -
- - - - - - - - - - - - - - - - - - - -
- - - - - - - - - - - - - - - - - - - -
- - - - - - - - - - - - - - - - - - - -

Plan to reality score: _ _ _ _ _ _ ./10

Progress towards goal

☐ last week ☐ this week ☐ remaining

"dreams DON'T WORK UNLESS you do"

⊛ Today I'm grateful for ...

- -

- -

- -

⛰ My goal: What are you looking toward?

- -

- -

◎ Today Targets: 30 Min. Time Blocks:

_____

- -

- -

_____

- -

- -

_____

- -

- -

☆ What will make today great?

- -

- -

- -

Plan to reality score: _ _ _ _ _ _ ./10

Progress towards goal

☐ last week   ☐ this week   ☐ remaining

"dreams DON'T WORK UNLESS you do"

(S) (M) (T) (W) (T) (F) (S)   /   /

⭐ Today I'm grateful for ...

🏔 My goal: What are you looking toward?

🎯 Today Targets: 30 Min. Time Blocks:

_____

_____

_____

🌟 What will make today great?

Plan to reality score: _ _ _ _ _ _ _ /10

Progress towards goal

☐ last week   ☐ this week   ☐ remaining

"dreams DONT WORK UNLESS you do"

(S) (M) (T) (W) (T) (F) (S)   /   /

⭐ Today I'm grateful for ...

------------------------------------   ------------------------------------
------------------------------------   ------------------------------------
------------------------------------   ------------------------------------
------------------------------------   ------------------------------------

🏔 My goal: What are you looking toward?

------------------------------------   ------------------------------------
------------------------------------   ------------------------------------
                                            ----

🎯 Today Targets: 30 Min. Time Blocks:

_____   ------------------------------------
------------------------------------   ------------------------------------
------------------------------------   ------------------------------------
_____   ------------------------------------
------------------------------------   ------------------------------------
------------------------------------   ------------------------------------
_____   ------------------------------------
------------------------------------   ------------------------------------
------------------------------------   ------------------------------------

🌟 What will make today great?

------------------------------------   ------------------------------------
------------------------------------   ------------------------------------
------------------------------------   ------------------------------------
------------------------------------   Plan to reality score: _ _ _ _ _ _ _ /10

Progress towards goal

☐ last week ☐ this week ☐ remaining

"dreams DONT WORK UNLESS you do"

HABIT TRACKER ◯ MOOD: 😊 🙂 😐 😟 ☹️ WIN THE DAY SCORE: / 10

(S) (M) (T) (W) (T) (F) (S)   /   /

⭐ Today I'm grateful for ...

_____

_____

_____

_____

🏔️ My goal: What are you looking toward?

_____

_____

_____

🎯 Today Targets: 30 Min. Time Blocks:

_____

_____

_____

_____

_____

_____

_____

_____

_____

_____

_____

_____

🌟 What will make today great?

_____

_____

_____

Plan to reality score: _ _ _ _ _ _ _ /10

Progress towards goal

☐ last week   ☐ this week   ☐ remaining

"dreams DONT WORK UNLESS you do"

(S) (M) (T) (W) (T) (F) (S)   /   /

⭐ Today I'm grateful for ...

🏁 My goal: What are you looking toward?

🎯 Today Targets: 30 Min. Time Blocks:

✨ What will make today great?

Progress towards goal

☐ last week ☐ this week ☐ remaining

"dreams
DONT WORK
UNLESS
you do"

HABIT TRACKER ◯   MOOD: 😊 🙂 😐 😟 ☹️   WIN THE DAY SCORE: / 10

Week Reflection

OUTCOME GOAL PROGRESS   % Completed ☑

1.—   20   40   60   80   100

2.—   20   40   60   80   100

3.—   20   40   60   80   100

What worked and what don't

+   —

 Moving forward, what things will you...

KEEP DOING

IMPROVE ON

START DOING

STOP ON

Who should thank / Ask for guidance moving forward:

Weekly Planning

TOP 3 WEEKLY OBJECTIVES: Est. Time ✓

1.—

2.—

3.—

EVENTS & DEADLINES:

OTHER TASKS / ERRANDS:

WEEK 8								WEEKLY REVIEW	
Day:								WK AVG	
WIN THE DAY SCORE									
PLAN TO REALITY									
BUCKET LIST COMPLETED:									

WEEKLY REFLECTION:
Lessons learned, highs, lows, memorable moments, etc.

_____
_____
_____
_____
_____
_____
_____
_____
_____
_____

What did your key relationships look like this week?

_____
_____
_____

How will I ensure next week is as good or better?

_____
_____
_____

(S) (M) (T) (W) (T) (F) (S)   /   /

⭐ Today I'm grateful for ...

- - - - - - - - - - - - - - - - - -

- - - - - - - - - - - - - - - - - -

- - - - - - - - - - - - - - - - - -

🏔️ My goal: What are you looking toward?

- - - - - - - - - - - - - - - - - -

- - - - - - - - - - - - - - - - - -

🎯 Today Targets: 30 Min. Time Blocks:

_____

- - - - - - - - - - - - - - - - - -

- - - - - - - - - - - - - - - - - -

_____

- - - - - - - - - - - - - - - - - -

- - - - - - - - - - - - - - - - - -

_____

- - - - - - - - - - - - - - - - - -

- - - - - - - - - - - - - - - - - -

🌟 What will make today great?

- - - - - - - - - - - - - - - - - -

- - - - - - - - - - - - - - - - - -

- - - - - - - - - - - - - - - - - -

- - - - - - - - - - - - - - - - - -

Plan to reality score: _ _ _ _ _ _ _ /10

Progress towards goal

☐ last week ☐ this week ☐ remaining

"*dreams* DON'T WORK UNLESS *you do*"

HABIT TRACKER ◯   MOOD: 😊 🙂 😐 😟 ☹️   WIN THE DAY SCORE: / 10

Today I'm grateful for ...

My goal: What are you looking toward?

Today Targets: 30 Min. Time Blocks:

What will make today great?

Plan to reality score: _ _ _ _ _ _ _ /10

Progress towards goal

☐ last week ☐ this week ☐ remaining

"dreams DONT WORK UNLESS you do"

HABIT TRACKER ◯   MOOD: ☺ ☺ ☺ ☺ ☹   WIN THE DAY SCORE: / 10

(S) (M) (T) (W) (T) (F) (S)　　/　　/

⭐ Today I'm grateful for ...

🏔 My goal:　　What are you looking toward?

🎯 Today Targets:　　30 Min. Time Blocks:

🌟 What will make today great?

Plan to reality score: _ _ _ _ _ /10

Progress towards goal

☐ last week ☐ this week ☐ remaining

"dreams
DONT WORK
UNLESS
you do"

(S) (M) (T) (W) (T) (F) (S)   /   /

⭐ Today I'm grateful for ...

🏔️ My goal: What are you looking toward?

🎯 Today Targets: 30 Min. Time Blocks:

_____

_____

_____

🌟 What will make today great?

Plan to reality score: _ _ _ _ _ /10

Progress towards goal

☐ last week ☐ this week ☐ remaining

"*dreams* DONT WORK UNLESS *you do*"

HABIT TRACKER ◯   MOOD: ☺ ☺ ☹ ☹ ☹   WIN THE DAY SCORE: / 10

(S) (M) (T) (W) (T) (F) (S) / /

Today I'm grateful for ...

My goal: What are you looking toward?

Today Targets: 30 Min. Time Blocks:

What will make today great?

Plan to reality score: _ _ _ _ _ _ _ /10

Progress towards goal

☐ last week ☐ this week ☐ remaining

"dreams DON'T WORK UNLESS you do"

HABIT TRACKER ◯   MOOD: ☺ ☺ ☺ ☹ ☹   WIN THE DAY SCORE: / 10

(S) (M) (T) (W) (T) (F) (S)   /   /

★ Today I'm grateful for ...

⚑ My goal: What are you looking toward?

◎ Today Targets: 30 Min. Time Blocks:

☆ What will make today great?

Progress towards goal

- [ ] last week
- [ ] this week
- [ ] remaining

"dreams DON'T WORK UNLESS you do"

(S) (M) (T) (W) (T) (F) (S)   /   /

⭐ Today I'm grateful for ...

- - - - - - - - - - - - - - - - - - -

- - - - - - - - - - - - - - - - - - -

- - - - - - - - - - - - - - - - - - -

🏔 My goal: What are you looking toward?

- - - - - - - - - - - - - - - - - - -

- - - - - - - - - - - - - - - - - - -

- - - - - - - - - - - - - - - - - - -

🎯 Today Targets: 30 Min. Time Blocks:

_____

- - - - - - - - - - - - - - - - - - -

- - - - - - - - - - - - - - - - - - -

_____

- - - - - - - - - - - - - - - - - - -

- - - - - - - - - - - - - - - - - - -

_____

- - - - - - - - - - - - - - - - - - -

- - - - - - - - - - - - - - - - - - -

🌟 What will make today great?

- - - - - - - - - - - - - - - - - - -

- - - - - - - - - - - - - - - - - - -

- - - - - - - - - - - - - - - - - - -

- - - - - - - - - - - - - - - - - - -

Plan to reality score: _ _ _ _ _ _ /10

Progress towards goal

☐ last week   ☐ this week   ☐ remaining

"dreams DONT WORK UNLESS you do"

Week Reflection

OUTCOME GOAL PROGRESS	% Completed ✓

1.-

20	40	60	80	100
●	●	●	●	●

2.-

20	40	60	80	100
●	●	●	●	●

3.-

20	40	60	80	100
●	●	●	●	●

What worked and what don't

+ —

Moving forward, what things will you...

KEEP DOING

IMPROVE ON

START DOING

STOP ON

Who should thank / Ask for guidance moving forward:

Weekly Planning

TOP 3 WEEKLY OBJECTIVES: Est. Time ☑

1.—

2.—

3.—

EVENTS & DEADLINES:

OTHER TASKS / ERRANDS:

"It's time for you to move,
realizing that the thing you are seeking is also seeking you."
- IYANLA VANZANT -

WEEK 8								WEEKLY REVIEW
Day:								WK AVG
WIN THE DAY SCORE								
PLAN TO REALITY								
BUCKET LIST COMPLETED:								

WEEKLY REFLECTION:
Lessons learned, highs, lows, memorable moments, etc.

What did your key relationships look like this week?

How will I ensure next week is as good or better?

Ⓢ Ⓜ Ⓣ Ⓦ Ⓣ Ⓕ Ⓢ   /   /

⭐ Today I'm grateful for ...

⛰ My goal: What are you looking toward?

🎯 Today Targets: 30 Min. Time Blocks:

🌟 What will make today great?

Progress towards goal

☐ last week   ☐ this week   ☐ remaining

"dreams DONT WORK UNLESS you do"

HABIT TRACKER ◯   MOOD: 😊 🙂 😐 😣 😞   WIN THE DAY SCORE: / 10

(S) (M) (T) (W) (T) (F) (S)   /   /

⭐ Today I'm grateful for ...

🏔 My goal: What are you looking toward?

🎯 Today Targets: 30 Min. Time Blocks:

🌟 What will make today great?

Plan to reality score: _ _ _ _ _ _ _ /10

Progress towards goal

☐ last week ☐ this week ☐ remaining

"dreams DONT WORK UNLESS you do"

HABIT TRACKER ○   MOOD: 😊 🙂 😐 😣 😫   WIN THE DAY SCORE: / 10

(S) (M) (T) (W) (T) (F) (S)   /   /

⭐ Today I'm grateful for …

-          -

-          -

-          -

-          -

🏔️ My goal: What are you looking toward?

-          -

-          -

-          -

🎯 Today Targets: 30 Min. Time Blocks:

_____   -

-          -

-          -

_____   -

-          -

-          -

_____   -

-          -

-          -

🌟 What will make today great?

-          -

-          -

-          -

-          Plan to reality score: _ _ _ _ _ _ ./10

Progress towards goal

☐ last week   ☐ this week   ☐ remaining

"*dreams* DON'T WORK UNLESS *you do*"

(S) (M) (T) (W) (T) (F) (S)   /   /

⭐ Today I'm grateful for ...

-     -

-     -

-     -

🏔️ My goal: What are you looking toward?

-     -

-     -

-     -

🎯 Today Targets: 30 Min. Time Blocks:

_____   -

-     -

-     -

_____   -

-     -

-     -

_____   -

-     -

-     -

🌟 What will make today great?

-     -

-     -

-     Plan to reality score: _ _ _ _ _ _ _ /10

Progress towards goal

☐ last week   ☐ this week   ☐ remaining

"dreams DONT WORK UNLESS you do"

(S) (M) (T) (W) (T) (F) (S)   /   /

⭐ Today I'm grateful for ...

🏔️ My goal: What are you looking toward?

🎯 Today Targets: 30 Min. Time Blocks:

✨ What will make today great?

Plan to reality score: _ _ _ _ _ _ /10

Progress towards goal

☐ last week ☐ this week ☐ remaining

"dreams DONT WORK UNLESS you do"

HABIT TRACKER ◯   MOOD: ☺ ☺ ☐ ☹ ☹   WIN THE DAY SCORE: / 10

⭐ Today I'm grateful for ...

🏔 My goal: What are you looking toward?

🎯 Today Targets: 30 Min. Time Blocks:

🌟 What will make today great?

Plan to reality score: _ _ _ _ _ _ /10

Progress towards goal

☐ last week ☐ this week ☐ remaining

"dreams DONT WORK UNLESS you do"

Ⓢ Ⓜ Ⓣ Ⓦ Ⓣ Ⓕ Ⓢ   /   /

✦ Today I'm grateful for ...

- -

- -

- -

My goal: What are you looking toward?

- -

- -

Today Targets: 30 Min. Time Blocks:

_____

- -

_____

- -

- -

_____

- -

- -

What will make today great?

- -

- -

- -

Plan to reality score: _ _ _ _ _ _ /10

Progress towards goal

☐ last week ☐ this week ☐ remaining

"dreams DONT WORK UNLESS you do"

Week Reflection

OUTCOME GOAL PROGRESS   % Completed ✓

	20	40	60	80	100
1.–	○	○	○	○	○

	20	40	60	80	100
2.–	○	○	○	○	○

	20	40	60	80	100
3.–	○	○	○	○	○

What worked and what don't

+ –

 Moving forward, what things will you...

KEEP DOING

IMPROVE ON

START DOING

STOP ON

Who should thank / Ask for guidance moving forward:

Weekly Planning

TOP 3 WEEKLY OBJECTIVES: Est. Time ☑

1.-

2.-

3.-

EVENTS & DEADLINES:

OTHER TASKS / ERRANDS:

WEEK 8									WEEKLY REVIEW
Day:									WK AVG
WIN THE DAY SCORE									
PLAN TO REALITY									
BUCKET LIST COMPLETED:									

WEEKLY REFLECTION:
Lessons learned, highs, lows, memorable moments, etc.

What did your key relationships look like this week?

How will I ensure next week is as good or better?

✦ Today I'm grateful for ...

🏔 My goal: What are you looking toward?

◎ Today Targets: 30 Min. Time Blocks:

☆ What will make today great?

Plan to reality score: _ _ _ _ _ _ /10

Progress towards goal

☐ last week ☐ this week ☐ remaining

"dreams DONT WORK UNLESS you do"

(S) (M) (T) (W) (T) (F) (S)   /   /

★ Today I'm grateful for ...

⛰ My goal: What are you looking toward?

◎ Today Targets: 30 Min. Time Blocks:

_____

_____

_____

☆ What will make today great?

Plan to reality score: _ _ _ _ _ _ _ /10

Progress towards goal

☐ last week ☐ this week ☐ remaining

"dreams DONT WORK UNLESS you do"

HABIT TRACKER ◯   MOOD: 😊 🙂 😐 😣 😠   WIN THE DAY SCORE: / 10

(S) (M) (T) (W) (T) (F) (S)   /   /

⭐ Today I'm grateful for ...

🏔 My goal: What are you looking toward?

🎯 Today Targets: 30 Min. Time Blocks:

🌟 What will make today great?

Plan to reality score: _ _ _ _ _ _ /10

Progress towards goal

☐ last week ☐ this week ☐ remaining

"dreams DON'T WORK UNLESS you do"

HABIT TRACKER ○   MOOD: 😊 🙂 😐 😣 ☹️   WIN THE DAY SCORE: / 10

(S) (M) (T) (W) (T) (F) (S)   /   /

⭐ Today I'm grateful for ...

🏔 My goal: What are you looking toward?

🎯 Today Targets: 30 Min. Time Blocks:

🌟 What will make today great?

Progress towards goal

☐ last week ☐ this week ☐ remaining

"*dreams* DONT WORK UNLESS *you do*"

⭐ Today I'm grateful for ...

🏔 My goal: What are you looking toward?

🎯 Today Targets: 30 Min. Time Blocks:

🌟 What will make today great?

Plan to reality score: _ _ _ _ _ _ _ /10

Progress towards goal

☐ last week ☐ this week ☐ remaining

"dreams
DONT WORK
UNLESS
you do"

(S) (M) (T) (W) (T) (F) (S)   /   /

⭐ Today I'm grateful for ...

-       -
-       -
-       -

🏔️ My goal: What are you looking toward?

-       -
-       -

🎯 Today Targets: 30 Min. Time Blocks:

_____   -
-       -
-       -
_____   -
-       -
_____   -
-       -
-       -

🌟 What will make today great?

-       -
-       -
-       -
-   Plan to reality score: _ _ _ _ _ _ /10

Progress towards goal

☐ last week ☐ this week ☐ remaining

"dreams DONT WORK UNLESS you do"

(S) (M) (T) (W) (T) (F) (S) / /

⭐ Today I'm grateful for ...

🏔️ My goal: What are you looking toward?

🎯 Today Targets: 30 Min. Time Blocks:

_____

_____

_____

🌟 What will make today great?

Plan to reality score: _ _ _ _ _ _ /10

Progress towards goal

☐ last week   ☐ this week   ☐ remaining

"dreams DON'T WORK UNLESS you do"

Week Reflection

OUTCOME GOAL PROGRESS

	% Completed ✓

1.–

20	40	60	80	100
●	●	●	●	●

2.–

20	40	60	80	100
●	●	●	●	●

3.–

20	40	60	80	100
●	●	●	●	●

What worked and what don't

+ –

 Moving forward, what things will you...

KEEP DOING

IMPROVE ON

START DOING

STOP ON

Who should thank / Ask for guidance moving forward:

Weekly Planning

TOP 3 WEEKLY OBJECTIVES: Est. Time ☑

1.-

2.-

3.-

EVENTS & DEADLINES:

OTHER TASKS / ERRANDS:

"Breathe. Let go. And remind yourself that this very moment is the only one you know you have for sure."

- OPRAH WINFREY -

WEEK 8								WEEKLY REVIEW
Day:								WK AVG
WIN THE DAY SCORE								
PLAN TO REALITY								
BUCKET LIST COMPLETED:								

WEEKLY REFLECTION:
Lessons learned, highs, lows, memorable moments, etc.

What did your key relationships look like this week?

How will I ensure next week is as good or better?

⊛ Today I'm grateful for ...

⛰ My goal: What are you looking toward?

◎ Today Targets: 30 Min. Time Blocks:

☆ What will make today great?

Plan to reality score: _ _ _ _ _ _ _ /10

Progress towards goal

☐ last week   ☐ this week   ☐ remaining

"dreams DONT WORK UNLESS you do"

(S) (M) (T) (W) (T) (F) (S)   /   /

⭐ Today I'm grateful for ...

🚩 My goal: What are you looking toward?

🎯 Today Targets: 30 Min. Time Blocks:

🌟 What will make today great?

Plan to reality score: _ _ _ _ _ _ ./10

Progress towards goal

☐ last week   ☐ this week   ☐ remaining

"dreams DONT WORK UNLESS you do"

(S) (M) (T) (W) (T) (F) (S)   /   /

⭐ Today I'm grateful for ...

🏔️ My goal: What are you looking toward?

🎯 Today Targets: 30 Min. Time Blocks:

🌟 What will make today great?

Progress towards goal

☐ last week ☐ this week ☐ remaining

"*dreams* DON'T WORK UNLESS *you do*"

HABIT TRACKER ◯   MOOD: 😊 🙂 😐 😣 ☹️   WIN THE DAY SCORE: / 10

(S) (M) (T) (W) (T) (F) (S) / /

⭐ Today I'm grateful for ...

🏔 My goal: What are you looking toward?

🎯 Today Targets: 30 Min. Time Blocks:

🌟 What will make today great?

Plan to reality score: _ _ _ _ _ _ /10

Progress towards goal

☐ last week   ☐ this week   ☐ remaining

"dreams DONT WORK UNLESS you do"

(S) (M) (T) (W) (T) (F) (S)   /   /

⭐ Today I'm grateful for ...

🚩 My goal: What are you looking toward?

🎯 Today Targets: 30 Min. Time Blocks:

⭐ What will make today great?

Plan to reality score: _ _ _ _ _ _ _ _ /10

Progress towards goal

- [ ] last week
- [ ] this week
- [ ] remaining

"*dreams* DON'T WORK UNLESS *you do*"

(S) (M) (T) (W) (T) (F) (S)   /   /

⭐ Today I'm grateful for ...

-     -
-     -
-     -
-     -

🏔 My goal: What are you looking toward?

-     -
-     -
-     -

🎯 Today Targets: 30 Min. Time Blocks:

_____   -
-     -
-     -
_____   -
-     -
-     -
_____   -
-     -
-     -

🌟 What will make today great?

-     -
-     -
-     -
-     Plan to reality score: _ _ _ _ _ /10

Progress towards goal

☐ last week   ☐ this week   ☐ remaining

"dreams DONT WORK UNLESS you do"

(S) (M) (T) (W) (T) (F) (S)   /   /

⊛ Today I'm grateful for ...

⛰ My goal: What are you looking toward?

◎ Today Targets: 30 Min. Time Blocks:

_____

_____

_____

☆ What will make today great?

Plan to reality score: _ _ _ _ _ _ /10

Progress towards goal

☐ last week   ☐ this week   ☐ remaining

"dreams DONT WORK UNLESS you do"

Week Reflection

OUTCOME GOAL PROGRESS	% Completed ✓

1.—

20	40	60	80	100
●	●	●	●	●

2.—

20	40	60	80	100
●	●	●	●	●

3.—

20	40	60	80	100
●	●	●	●	●

What worked and what don't

+ —

 Moving forward, what things will you...

KEEP DOING

IMPROVE ON

START DOING

STOP ON

Who should thank / Ask for guidance moving forward:

Weekly Planning

TOP 3 WEEKLY OBJECTIVES: Est. Time ✓

1.—

2.—

3.—

EVENTS & DEADLINES:

OTHER TASKS / ERRANDS:

*"You are on the eve of a complete victory.
You can't go wrong. The world is behind you."*
- JOSEPHINE BAKER -

WEEK 8 — WEEKLY REVIEW

Day:								WK AVG
WIN THE DAY SCORE								
PLAN TO REALITY								
BUCKET LIST COMPLETED:								

WEEKLY REFLECTION:
Lessons learned, highs, lows, memorable moments, etc.

What did your key relationships look like this week?

How will I ensure next week is as good or better?

(S) (M) (T) (W) (T) (F) (S)   /   /

⭐ Today I'm grateful for ...

_____   _____
_____   _____
_____   _____
_____   _____

🏔 My goal: What are you looking toward?

_____   _____
_____   _____
_____   _____

🎯 Today Targets: 30 Min. Time Blocks:

_____   _____
_____   _____
_____   _____
_____   _____
_____   _____
_____   _____
_____   _____
_____   _____

🌟 What will make today great?

_____   _____
_____   _____
_____   _____

Plan to reality score: _ _ _ _ _ _ /10

Progress towards goal

☐ last week ☐ this week ☐ remaining

"dreams DONT WORK UNLESS you do"

(S) (M) (T) (W) (T) (F) (S)   /   /

⭐ Today I'm grateful for ...

- -

- -

- -

🚩 My goal: What are you looking toward?

- -

- -

🎯 Today Targets: 30 Min. Time Blocks:

_____

- -

- -

_____

- -

- -

_____

- -

- -

🌟 What will make today great?

- -

- -

- -

Plan to reality score: _ _ _ _ _ _ _ /10

Progress towards goal

☐ last week   ☐ this week   ☐ remaining

"dreams DON'T WORK UNLESS you do"

HABIT TRACKER ○   MOOD: ☺ ☺ ☺ ☺ ☹   WIN THE DAY SCORE: / 10

(S) (M) (T) (W) (T) (F) (S)   /   /

⭐ Today I'm grateful for ...

🏔 My goal: What are you looking toward?

🎯 Today Targets: 30 Min. Time Blocks:

_____

_____

_____

🌟 What will make today great?

Plan to reality score: _ _ _ _ _ _ /10

Progress towards goal

☐ last week ☐ this week ☐ remaining

"dreams DONT WORK UNLESS you do"

HABIT TRACKER ○   MOOD: ☺ ☺ ☺ ☹ ☹   WIN THE DAY SCORE: / 10

(S) (M) (T) (W) (T) (F) (S)   /   /

⭐ Today I'm grateful for ...

🏔 My goal: What are you looking toward?

🎯 Today Targets: 30 Min. Time Blocks:

🌟 What will make today great?

Plan to reality score: _ _ _ _ _ _ /10

Progress towards goal

☐ last week   ☐ this week   ☐ remaining

"dreams DON'T WORK UNLESS you do"

(S) (M) (T) (W) (T) (F) (S) / /

★ Today I'm grateful for ...

🏔 My goal: What are you looking toward?

◎ Today Targets: 30 Min. Time Blocks:

☆ What will make today great?

Progress towards goal

☐ last week ☐ this week ☐ remaining

"dreams
DONT WORK
UNLESS
you do"

HABIT TRACKER ○   MOOD: 😊 🙂 😐 😕 ☹️   WIN THE DAY SCORE: / 10

⊛ Today I'm grateful for ...

⛰ My goal: What are you looking toward?

◎ Today Targets: 30 Min. Time Blocks:

✦ What will make today great?

Plan to reality score: _____ /10

Progress towards goal

☐ last week   ☐ this week   ☐ remaining

"dreams DONT WORK UNLESS you do"

(S) (M) (T) (W) (T) (F) (S) / /

⭐ Today I'm grateful for ...

🏔 My goal: What are you looking toward?

🎯 Today Targets: 30 Min. Time Blocks:

🌟 What will make today great?

Plan to reality score: _ _ _ _ _ _ _ /10

Progress towards goal

☐ last week ☐ this week ☐ remaining

"dreams
DONT WORK
UNLESS
you do"

Week Reflection

OUTCOME GOAL PROGRESS		% Completed ✓

	20	40	60	80	100
1.-	○	○	○	○	○

	20	40	60	80	100
2.-	○	○	○	○	○

	20	40	60	80	100
3.-	○	○	○	○	○

What worked and what don't

+ −

 Moving forward, what things will you...

KEEP DOING

IMPROVE ON

START DOING

STOP ON

Who should thank / Ask for guidance moving forward:

Weekly Planning

TOP 3 WEEKLY OBJECTIVES: Est. Time ☑

1.—

2.—

3.—

EVENTS & DEADLINES:

OTHER TASKS / ERRANDS:

"Don't wait around for other people to be happy for you. Any happiness you get you've got to make yourself."
— ALICE WALKER -

WEEK 8								WEEKLY REVIEW
Day:								WK AVG
WIN THE DAY SCORE								
PLAN TO REALITY								
BUCKET LIST COMPLETED:								

WEEKLY REFLECTION:
Lessons learned, highs, lows, memorable moments, etc.

What did your key relationships look like this week?

How will I ensure next week is as good or better?

(S) (M) (T) (W) (T) (F) (S) / /

★ Today I'm grateful for ...

⛰ My goal: What are you looking toward?

◎ Today Targets: 30 Min. Time Blocks:

☆ What will make today great?

Progress towards goal

☐ last week ☐ this week ☐ remaining

"dreams
DONT WORK
UNLESS
you do"

HABIT TRACKER ○   MOOD: 😊 🙂 😐 😟 ☹️   WIN THE DAY SCORE: / 10

(S) (M) (T) (W) (T) (F) (S)   /   /

★ Today I'm grateful for ...

⚑ My goal: What are you looking toward?

◎ Today Targets: 30 Min. Time Blocks:

☆ What will make today great?

Plan to reality score: _ _ _ _ _ _ _ ./10

Progress towards goal

☐ last week   ☐ this week   ☐ remaining

"dreams DONT WORK UNLESS you do"

HABIT TRACKER ○   MOOD: 😊 🙂 😐 😟 ☹️   WIN THE DAY SCORE: / 10

(S) (M) (T) (W) (T) (F) (S)   /   /

⭐ Today I'm grateful for ...

🚩 My goal: What are you looking toward?

🎯 Today Targets: 30 Min. Time Blocks:

✨ What will make today great?

Progress towards goal

☐ last week   ☐ this week   ☐ remaining

"dreams DONT WORK UNLESS you do"

⭐ Today I'm grateful for ...

🏔 My goal: What are you looking toward?

🎯 Today Targets: 30 Min. Time Blocks:

🌟 What will make today great?

Plan to reality score: _ _ _ _ _ /10

Progress towards goal

☐ last week   ☐ this week   ☐ remaining

"dreams DONT WORK UNLESS you do"

HABIT TRACKER ○   MOOD: 😊 🙂 😐 😟 ☹️   WIN THE DAY SCORE: / 10

(S) (M) (T) (W) (T) (F) (S)   /   /

⭐ Today I'm grateful for ...

🏔️ My goal: What are you looking toward?

🎯 Today Targets: 30 Min. Time Blocks:

_____

_____

_____

🌟 What will make today great?

Plan to reality score: _ _ _ _ _ _ /10

Progress towards goal

☐ last week ☐ this week ☐ remaining

"dreams DONT WORK UNLESS you do"

⭐ Today I'm grateful for ...

🏔 My goal: What are you looking toward?

🎯 Today Targets: 30 Min. Time Blocks:

🌟 What will make today great?

Progress towards goal

☐ last week   ☐ this week   ☐ remaining

"*dreams* DONT WORK UNLESS *you do*"

(S) (M) (T) (W) (T) (F) (S)   /   /

⭐ Today I'm grateful for ...

🚩 My goal: What are you looking toward?

🎯 Today Targets: 30 Min. Time Blocks:

🌟 What will make today great?

Progress towards goal

☐ last week ☐ this week ☐ remaining

"*dreams* DON'T WORK UNLESS *you do*"

Week Reflection

OUTCOME GOAL PROGRESS	% Completed ✓

1.–   20 ○   40 ○   60 ○   80 ○   100 ○

2.–   20 ○   40 ○   60 ○   80 ○   100 ○

3.–   20 ○   40 ○   60 ○   80 ○   100 ○

What worked and what don't

+   –

 Moving forward, what things will you...

KEEP DOING

IMPROVE ON

START DOING

STOP ON

Who should thank / Ask for guidance moving forward:

Weekly Planning

TOP 3 WEEKLY OBJECTIVES: Est. Time ✓

1.–

2.–

3.–

EVENTS & DEADLINES:

OTHER TASKS / ERRANDS:

WEEK 8								WEEKLY REVIEW
Day:								WK AVG
WIN THE DAY SCORE								
PLAN TO REALITY								
BUCKET LIST COMPLETED:								

WEEKLY REFLECTION:
Lessons learned, highs, lows, memorable moments, etc.

What did your key relationships look like this week?

How will I ensure next week is as good or better?

⊛ Today I'm grateful for ...

⛰ My goal: What are you looking toward?

⊚ Today Targets: 30 Min. Time Blocks:

✶ What will make today great?

Plan to reality score: _____ /10

Progress towards goal

☐ last week ☐ this week ☐ remaining

"dreams DONT WORK UNLESS you do"

HABIT TRACKER ○   MOOD: 😊 🙂 😐 😣 😫   WIN THE DAY SCORE: / 10

(S) (M) (T) (W) (T) (F) (S)   /   /

⭐ Today I'm grateful for ...

🚩 My goal: What are you looking toward?

🎯 Today Targets: 30 Min. Time Blocks:

_____

_____

_____

🌟 What will make today great?

Plan to reality score: _ _ _ _ _ _ _ /10

Progress towards goal

☐ last week ☐ this week ☐ remaining

"dreams DONT WORK UNLESS you do"

(S) (M) (T) (W) (T) (F) (S)   /   /

⭐ Today I'm grateful for ...

------------------------------------   ------------------------------------
------------------------------------   ------------------------------------
------------------------------------   ------------------------------------
------------------------------------   ------------------------------------

🏔️ My goal: What are you looking toward?

------------------------------------   ------------------------------------
------------------------------------   ------------------------------------
------------------------------------   ------------------------------------

🎯 Today Targets: 30 Min. Time Blocks:

_____   ------------------------------------
------------------------------------   ------------------------------------
------------------------------------   ------------------------------------
------------------------------------   ------------------------------------
_____   ------------------------------------
------------------------------------   ------------------------------------
------------------------------------   ------------------------------------
_____   ------------------------------------
------------------------------------   ------------------------------------
------------------------------------   ------------------------------------

🌟 What will make today great?

------------------------------------   ------------------------------------
------------------------------------   ------------------------------------
------------------------------------   ------------------------------------
------------------------------------   Plan to reality score: _ _ _ _ _ _ ./10

Progress towards goal

☐ last week ☐ this week ☐ remaining

"dreams DONT WORK UNLESS you do"

(S) (M) (T) (W) (T) (F) (S) / /

⭐ Today I'm grateful for ...

🚩 My goal: What are you looking toward?

🎯 Today Targets: 30 Min. Time Blocks:

✨ What will make today great?

Plan to reality score: _ _ _ _ _ _ /10

Progress towards goal

☐ last week ☐ this week ☐ remaining

"dreams DON'T WORK UNLESS you do"

HABIT TRACKER ◯   MOOD: 😀 🙂 😐 😟 ☹️   WIN THE DAY SCORE: / 10

(S) (M) (T) (W) (T) (F) (S) / /

★ Today I'm grateful for ...

⛰ My goal: What are you looking toward?

◎ Today Targets: 30 Min. Time Blocks:

☆ What will make today great?

Progress towards goal

☐ last week   ☐ this week   ☐ remaining

"dreams
DONT WORK
UNLESS
you do"

⭐ Today I'm grateful for ...

-   -

-   -

-   -

🏔 My goal: What are you looking toward?

-   -

-   -

🎯 Today Targets: 30 Min. Time Blocks:

_____   -

-   -

-   -

_____   -

-   -

_____   -

-   -

-   -

🌟 What will make today great?

-   -

-   -

-   Plan to reality score: _ _ _ _ _ _ _ /10

Progress towards goal

☐ last week ☐ this week ☐ remaining

"dreams DONT WORK UNLESS you do"

⭐ Today I'm grateful for ...

- - - - - - - - - - - - - - - - - - -

- - - - - - - - - - - - - - - - - - -

🏔 My goal: What are you looking toward?

- - - - - - - - - - - - - - - - - - -

- - - - - - - - - - - - - - - - - - -

🎯 Today Targets: 30 Min. Time Blocks:

_____

- - - - - - - - - - - - - - - - - - -

- - - - - - - - - - - - - - - - - - -

- - - - - - - - - - - - - - - - - - -

_____

- - - - - - - - - - - - - - - - - - -

- - - - - - - - - - - - - - - - - - -

_____

- - - - - - - - - - - - - - - - - - -

- - - - - - - - - - - - - - - - - - -

🌟 What will make today great?

- - - - - - - - - - - - - - - - - - -

- - - - - - - - - - - - - - - - - - -

- - - - - - - - - - - - - - - - - - -

Plan to reality score: _ _ _ _ _ _ /10

Progress towards goal

☐ last week   ☐ this week   ☐ remaining

"dreams DON'T WORK UNLESS you do"

Week Reflection

OUTCOME GOAL PROGRESS

% Completed ✓

	20	40	60	80	100

1.— ⚫ ⚫ ⚫ ⚫ ⚫

2.— ⚫ ⚫ ⚫ ⚫ ⚫

3.— ⚫ ⚫ ⚫ ⚫ ⚫

What worked and what don't

+ —

Moving forward, what things will you...

KEEP DOING

- -
- -
- -
- -
- -
- -
- -
- -
- -

IMPROVE ON

- -
- -
- -
- -
- -
- -
- -
- -
- -

START DOING

- -
- -
- -
- -
- -
- -
- -
- -

STOP ON

- -
- -
- -
- -
- -
- -
- -
- -

Who should thank / Ask for guidance moving forward:

- -
- -
- -

Weekly Planning

TOP 3 WEEKLY OBJECTIVES: Est. Time ✓

1.—

2.—

3.—

EVENTS & DEADLINES:

OTHER TASKS / ERRANDS:

"I don't have to go around trying to save everybody anymore;
that's not my job. "
-JADA PINKETT SMITH -

WEEK 8								WEEKLY REVIEW
Day:								WK AVG
WIN THE DAY SCORE								
PLAN TO REALITY								
BUCKET LIST COMPLETED:								

WEEKLY REFLECTION:
Lessons learned, highs, lows, memorable moments, etc.

What did your key relationships look like this week?

How will I ensure next week is as good or better?

(S) (M) (T) (W) (T) (F) (S)   /   /

⭐ Today I'm grateful for ...

🏔️ My goal: What are you looking toward?

🎯 Today Targets: 30 Min. Time Blocks:

✨ What will make today great?

Progress towards goal

☐ last week ☐ this week ☐ remaining

"dreams DON'T WORK UNLESS you do"

(S) (M) (T) (W) (T) (F) (S)   /   /

⭐ Today I'm grateful for ...

🏔 My goal: What are you looking toward?

🎯 Today Targets: 30 Min. Time Blocks:

🌟 What will make today great?

Progress towards goal

☐ last week ☐ this week ☐ remaining

"dreams DON'T WORK UNLESS you do"

HABIT TRACKER ◯   MOOD: 😊 🙂 😐 😟 ☹️   WIN THE DAY SCORE: / 10

(S) (M) (T) (W) (T) (F) (S) / /

⭐ Today I'm grateful for ...

🏔 My goal: What are you looking toward?

🎯 Today Targets: 30 Min. Time Blocks:

🖐⭐ What will make today great?

Progress towards goal

☐ last week   ☐ this week   ☐ remaining

"dreams DONT WORK UNLESS you do"

⭐ Today I'm grateful for ...

- - - - - - - - - - - - - - - - - - - -

- - - - - - - - - - - - - - - - - - - -

- - - - - - - - - - - - - - - - - - - -

🏔 My goal: What are you looking toward?

- - - - - - - - - - - - - - - - - - - -

- - - - - - - - - - - - - - - - - - - -

🎯 Today Targets: 30 Min. Time Blocks:

_____

- - - - - - - - - - - - - - - - - - - -

- - - - - - - - - - - - - - - - - - - -

_____

- - - - - - - - - - - - - - - - - - - -

- - - - - - - - - - - - - - - - - - - -

_____

- - - - - - - - - - - - - - - - - - - -

🌟 What will make today great?

- - - - - - - - - - - - - - - - - - - -

- - - - - - - - - - - - - - - - - - - -

- - - - - - - - - - - - - - - - - - - -

Plan to reality score: _ _ _ _ _ _ _ /10

Progress towards goal

☐ last week   ☐ this week   ☐ remaining

"dreams
DONT WORK
UNLESS
you do"

(S) (M) (T) (W) (T) (F) (S)   /   /

⭐ Today I'm grateful for ...

- -

- -

- -

🏔️ My goal: What are you looking toward?

- -

- -

🎯 Today Targets: 30 Min. Time Blocks:

_____

- -

- -

_____

- -

- -

_____

- -

- -

🌟 What will make today great?

- -

- -

- -

- -

Plan to reality score: _ _ _ _ _ _ _ /10

Progress towards goal

☐ last week ☐ this week ☐ remaining

"dreams DON'T WORK UNLESS you do"

(S) (M) (T) (W) (T) (F) (S)   /   /

⭐ Today I'm grateful for ...

🏔 My goal: What are you looking toward?

🎯 Today Targets: 30 Min. Time Blocks:

🌟 What will make today great?

Plan to reality score: _ _ _ _ _ ./10

Progress towards goal

☐ last week   ☐ this week   ☐ remaining

"dreams DON'T WORK UNLESS you do"

HABIT TRACKER ○   MOOD: 😀 🙂 😐 😟 ☹️   WIN THE DAY SCORE: / 10

⭐ Today I'm grateful for ...

⛰️ My goal: What are you looking toward?

🎯 Today Targets: 30 Min. Time Blocks:

🌟 What will make today great?

Plan to reality score: _ _ _ _ _ _ _ /10

Progress towards goal

☐ last week ☐ this week ☐ remaining

"dreams DONT WORK UNLESS you do"

Week Reflection

OUTCOME GOAL PROGRESS	% Completed ✓

1.—   20 ●   40 ●   60 ●   80 ●   100 ●

2.—   20 ●   40 ●   60 ●   80 ●   100 ●

3.—   20 ●   40 ●   60 ●   80 ●   100 ●

What worked and what don't

+   —

 Moving forward, what things will you...

KEEP DOING

IMPROVE ON

START DOING

STOP ON

Who should thank / Ask for guidance moving forward:

Weekly Planning

TOP 3 WEEKLY OBJECTIVES:

Est. Time ✓

1.-

2.-

3.-

EVENTS & DEADLINES:

OTHER TASKS / ERRANDS:

> *"It isn't where you come from; it's where you're going that counts."*
> - ELLA FITZGERALD -

WEEK 8								WEEKLY REVIEW	
Day:								WK AVG	
WIN THE DAY SCORE									
PLAN TO REALITY									
BUCKET LIST COMPLETED:									

WEEKLY REFLECTION:
Lessons learned, highs, lows, memorable moments, etc.

What did your key relationships look like this week?

How will I ensure next week is as good or better?

⭐ Today I'm grateful for ...

🏔 My goal: What are you looking toward?

🎯 Today Targets: 30 Min. Time Blocks:

⭐ What will make today great?

Plan to reality score: _ _ _ _ _ _ _ . /10

Progress towards goal

☐ last week ☐ this week ☐ remaining

"*dreams* DON'T WORK UNLESS *you do*"

(S) (M) (T) (W) (T) (F) (S) / /

⭐ Today I'm grateful for ...

🏔️ My goal: What are you looking toward?

🎯 Today Targets: 30 Min. Time Blocks:

_____

_____

_____

🌟 What will make today great?

Plan to reality score: _ _ _ _ _ _ /10

Progress towards goal

☐ last week   ☐ this week   ☐ remaining

"dreams DONT WORK UNLESS you do"

✦ Today I'm grateful for ...

⛰ My goal: What are you looking toward?

◎ Today Targets: 30 Min. Time Blocks:

☆ What will make today great?

Plan to reality score: _ _ _ _ _ _ /10

Progress towards goal

☐ last week ☐ this week ☐ remaining

"dreams DONT WORK UNLESS you do"

HABIT TRACKER ◯   MOOD: 😊 🙂 😐 😣 😞   WIN THE DAY SCORE: / 10

(S) (M) (T) (W) (T) (F) (S)   /   /

⭐ Today I'm grateful for ...

_____

_____

_____

_____

🏔 My goal: What are you looking toward?

_____

_____

🎯 Today Targets: 30 Min. Time Blocks:

_____

_____

_____

_____

_____

_____

🌟 What will make today great?

_____

_____

_____

Plan to reality score: _ _ _ _ _ _ _ /10

Progress towards goal

☐ last week   ☐ this week   ☐ remaining

"dreams DONT WORK UNLESS you do"

✦ Today I'm grateful for ...

⛰ My goal: What are you looking toward?

◎ Today Targets: 30 Min. Time Blocks:

✧ What will make today great?

Plan to reality score: _ _ _ _ _ _ /10

Progress towards goal

☐ last week   ☐ this week   ☐ remaining

"dreams DONT WORK UNLESS you do"

(S) (M) (T) (W) (T) (F) (S) / /

⬡ Today I'm grateful for ...

⛰ My goal: What are you looking toward?

◎ Today Targets: 30 Min. Time Blocks:

_____

_____

_____

☆ What will make today great?

Plan to reality score: _____ /10

Progress towards goal

☐ last week ☐ this week ☐ remaining

"dreams DONT WORK UNLESS you do"

HABIT TRACKER ◯   MOOD: 😊 🙂 😐 😟 ☹️   WIN THE DAY SCORE: / 10

(S) (M) (T) (W) (T) (F) (S)   /   /

⭐ Today I'm grateful for ...

🏔 My goal: What are you looking toward?

🎯 Today Targets: 30 Min. Time Blocks:

_____

_____

_____

🌟 What will make today great?

Plan to reality score:_____./10

Progress towards goal

☐ last week   ☐ this week   ☐ remaining

"dreams DONT WORK UNLESS you do"

Week Reflection

OUTCOME GOAL PROGRESS	% Completed ☑

1.—   20   40   60   80   100

2.—   20   40   60   80   100

3.—   20   40   60   80   100

What worked and what don't

+ —

Moving forward, what things will you...

KEEP DOING

IMPROVE ON

START DOING

STOP ON

Who should thank / Ask for guidance moving forward:

Weekly Planning

TOP 3 WEEKLY OBJECTIVES: Est. Time ✓

1.-

2.-

3.-

EVENTS & DEADLINES:

OTHER TASKS / ERRANDS:

> "My mission in life is not merely to survive, but to thrive; and to do so with some passion, some compassion, some humor, and some style."
> - MAYA ANGELOU -

WEEK 8								WEEKLY REVIEW
Day:								WK AVG
WIN THE DAY SCORE								
PLAN TO REALITY								
BUCKET LIST COMPLETED:								

WEEKLY REFLECTION:
Lessons learned, highs, lows, memorable moments, etc.

What did your key relationships look like this week?

How will I ensure next week is as good or better?

(S) (M) (T) (W) (T) (F) (S)   /   /

⭐ Today I'm grateful for ...

- -
- -
- -

🏔️ My goal: What are you looking toward?

- -
- -

🎯 Today Targets: 30 Min. Time Blocks:

_____

- -
- -

_____

- -
- -

_____

- -
- -

🌟 What will make today great?

- -
- -
- -

Plan to reality score: _ _ _ _ _ _ /10

Progress towards goal

☐ last week ☐ this week ☐ remaining

"*dreams* DONT WORK UNLESS *you do*"

(S) (M) (T) (W) (T) (F) (S)   /   /

⭐ Today I'm grateful for ...

🏔️ My goal: What are you looking toward?

🎯 Today Targets: 30 Min. Time Blocks:

_____

_____

_____

🌟 What will make today great?

Plan to reality score: _ _ _ _ _ _ _ ./10

Progress towards goal

☐ last week   ☐ this week   ☐ remaining

"dreams DONT WORK UNLESS you do"

(S) (M) (T) (W) (T) (F) (S) / /

⭐ Today I'm grateful for ...

🏔 My goal: What are you looking toward?

🎯 Today Targets: 30 Min. Time Blocks:

⭐ What will make today great?

Plan to reality score: _ _ _ _ _ _ _ /10

Progress towards goal

☐ last week ☐ this week ☐ remaining

"*dreams* DONT WORK UNLESS *you do*"

(S) (M) (T) (W) (T) (F) (S)   /   /

⭐ Today I'm grateful for ...

🏔 My goal: What are you looking toward?

🎯 Today Targets: 30 Min. Time Blocks:

✨ What will make today great?

Progress towards goal

☐ last week ☐ this week ☐ remaining

"dreams DONT WORK UNLESS you do"

⭐ Today I'm grateful for ...

🚩 My goal: What are you looking toward?

🎯 Today Targets: 30 Min. Time Blocks:

🌟 What will make today great?

Plan to reality score: _ _ _ _ _ _ _ /10

Progress towards goal

☐ last week ☐ this week ☐ remaining

"dreams DON'T WORK UNLESS you do"

✪ Today I'm grateful for ...

⛰ My goal: What are you looking toward?

◎ Today Targets: 30 Min. Time Blocks:

_____

_____

_____

✩ What will make today great?

Plan to reality score: _ _ _ _ _ _ /10

Progress towards goal

☐ last week ☐ this week ☐ remaining

"dreams DON'T WORK UNLESS you do"

⭐ Today I'm grateful for ...

🏔 My goal: What are you looking toward?

🎯 Today Targets: 30 Min. Time Blocks:

⭐ What will make today great?

Plan to reality score: _ _ _ _ _ _ /10

Progress towards goal

☐ last week ☐ this week ☐ remaining

"*dreams* DONT WORK UNLESS *you do*"

HABIT TRACKER ○   MOOD: 😄 🙂 😐 😟 ☹   WIN THE DAY SCORE: / 10

Week Reflection

OUTCOME GOAL PROGRESS	% Completed ✓

1.-
| 20 | 40 | 60 | 80 | 100 |
| ● | ● | ● | ● | ● |

2.-
| 20 | 40 | 60 | 80 | 100 |
| ● | ● | ● | ● | ● |

3.-
| 20 | 40 | 60 | 80 | 100 |
| ● | ● | ● | ● | ● |

What worked and what don't

+ —

Moving forward, what things will you...

KEEP DOING

- -
- -
- -
- -
- -
- -
- -
- -
- -

IMPROVE ON

- -
- -
- -
- -
- -
- -
- -
- -
- -

START DOING

- -
- -
- -
- -
- -
- -
- -
- -
- -

STOP ON

- -
- -
- -
- -
- -
- -
- -
- -
- -

Who should thank / Ask for guidance moving forward:

- -
- -
- -

Weekly Planning

TOP 3 WEEKLY OBJECTIVES: Est. Time ✓

1.-

2.-

3.-

EVENTS & DEADLINES:

OTHER TASKS / ERRANDS:

"I am lucky that whatever fear I have inside me,
my desire to win is always stronger."
- SERENA WILLIAMS -

WEEK 8							WEEKLY REVIEW
Day:							WK AVG
WIN THE DAY SCORE							
PLAN TO REALITY							
BUCKET LIST COMPLETED:							

WEEKLY REFLECTION:
Lessons learned, highs, lows, memorable moments, etc.

- -
- -
- -
- -
- -
- -
- -
- -
- -

What did your key relationships look like this week?

- -
- -
- -

How will I ensure next week is as good or better?

- -
- -
- -

(S) (M) (T) (W) (T) (F) (S) / /

⭐ Today I'm grateful for ...

🏔 My goal: What are you looking toward?

🎯 Today Targets: 30 Min. Time Blocks:

_____

_____

_____

🌟 What will make today great?

Progress towards goal

☐ last week ☐ this week ☐ remaining

"dreams DONT WORK UNLESS you do"

HABIT TRACKER ◯   MOOD: ☺ ☺ ☺ ☹ ☹   WIN THE DAY SCORE: / 10

(S) (M) (T) (W) (T) (F) (S)   /   /

⭐ Today I'm grateful for ...

🏔 My goal: What are you looking toward?

🎯 Today Targets: 30 Min. Time Blocks:

⭐ What will make today great?

Plan to reality score: _____ /10

Progress towards goal

☐ last week   ☐ this week   ☐ remaining

"dreams DONT WORK UNLESS you do"

(S) (M) (T) (W) (T) (F) (S)   /   /

⭐ Today I'm grateful for ...

- - - - - - - - - - - - - - - -   -
- - - - - - - - - - - - - - - -   -
- - - - - - - - - - - - - - - -   -
- - - - - - - - - - - - - - - -   -

🏔️ My goal: What are you looking toward?

- - - - - - - - - - - - - - - -   -
- - - - - - - - - - - - - - - -   -
- - - - - - - - - - - - - - - -   -

🎯 Today Targets: 30 Min. Time Blocks:

_____   -
- - - - - - - - - - - - - - - -   -
- - - - - - - - - - - - - - - -   -
- - - - - - - - - - - - - - - -   -
_____   -
- - - - - - - - - - - - - - - -   -
- - - - - - - - - - - - - - - -   -
_____   -
- - - - - - - - - - - - - - - -   -
- - - - - - - - - - - - - - - -   -

🌟 What will make today great?

- - - - - - - - - - - - - - - -   -
- - - - - - - - - - - - - - - -   -
- - - - - - - - - - - - - - - -   -
- - - - - - - - - - - - - - - -

Plan to reality score: _ _ _ _ _ _ ./10

Progress towards goal

☐ last week   ☐ this week   ☐ remaining

"dreams DONT WORK UNLESS you do"

⭐ Today I'm grateful for ...

🏔️ My goal: What are you looking toward?

🎯 Today Targets: 30 Min. Time Blocks:

✨ What will make today great?

Plan to reality score: _ _ _ _ _ _ ./10

Progress towards goal

☐ last week   ☐ this week   ☐ remaining

"dreams DONT WORK UNLESS you do"

(S) (M) (T) (W) (T) (F) (S)   /   /

⭐ Today I'm grateful for ...

🏔 My goal: What are you looking toward?

🎯 Today Targets: 30 Min. Time Blocks:

_____

_____

_____

🌟 What will make today great?

Plan to reality score: _ _ _ _ _ _ _ /10

Progress towards goal

☐ last week ☐ this week ☐ remaining

"dreams DONT WORK UNLESS you do"

(S) (M) (T) (W) (T) (F) (S)   /   /

☆ Today I'm grateful for ...

⛰ My goal: What are you looking toward?

◎ Today Targets: 30 Min. Time Blocks:

_____

_____

_____

☆ What will make today great?

Plan to reality score: _ _ _ _ _ _ /10

Progress towards goal

☐ last week ☐ this week ☐ remaining

"dreams DON'T WORK UNLESS you do"

HABIT TRACKER ◯   MOOD: ☺ ☺ ☺ ☹ ☹   WIN THE DAY SCORE: / 10

(S) (M) (T) (W) (T) (F) (S)   /   /

⭐ Today I'm grateful for ...

🏔 My goal: What are you looking toward?

🎯 Today Targets: 30 Min. Time Blocks:

_____

_____

_____

🌟 What will make today great?

Progress towards goal

☐ last week ☐ this week ☐ remaining

"dreams DON'T WORK UNLESS you do"

Week Reflection

OUTCOME GOAL PROGRESS	% Completed ✓

1.—

20	40	60	80	100
○	○	○	○	○

2.—

20	40	60	80	100
○	○	○	○	○

3.—

20	40	60	80	100
○	○	○	○	○

What worked and what don't

+ —

Moving forward, what things will you...

KEEP DOING

- -
- -
- -
- -
- -
- -
- -
- -
- -
- -

IMPROVE ON

- -
- -
- -
- -
- -
- -
- -
- -
- -
- -

START DOING

- -
- -
- -
- -
- -
- -
- -
- -
- -
- -

STOP ON

- -
- -
- -
- -
- -
- -
- -
- -
- -
- -

Who should thank / Ask for guidance moving forward:

- -
- -
- -

Weekly Planning

TOP 3 WEEKLY OBJECTIVES: Est. Time ✓

1.—

2.—

3.—

EVENTS & DEADLINES:

OTHER TASKS / ERRANDS:

"You've just got to follow your own path. You have to trust your heart and you have to listen to the warnings."
— CHAKA KHAN —

WEEK 8								WEEKLY REVIEW
Day:								WK AVG
WIN THE DAY SCORE								
PLAN TO REALITY								
BUCKET LIST COMPLETED:								

WEEKLY REFLECTION:
Lessons learned, highs, lows, memorable moments, etc.

_____
_____
_____
_____
_____
_____
_____
_____
_____

What did your key relationships look like this week?

_____
_____
_____

How will I ensure next week is as good or better?

_____
_____
_____

⊛ Today I'm grateful for ...

🏔 My goal: What are you looking toward?

◎ Today Targets: 30 Min. Time Blocks:

_____

_____

_____

☆ What will make today great?

Progress towards goal

☐ last week ☐ this week ☐ remaining

"dreams DON'T WORK UNLESS you do"

(S) (M) (T) (W) (T) (F) (S)   /   /

⭐ Today I'm grateful for ...

🏔️ My goal: What are you looking toward?

🎯 Today Targets: 30 Min. Time Blocks:

🌟 What will make today great?

Progress towards goal

☐ last week   ☐ this week   ☐ remaining

"dreams DONT WORK UNLESS you do"

(S) (M) (T) (W) (T) (F) (S)   /   /

⭐ Today I'm grateful for ...

- - - - - - - - - - - - - - - -

- - - - - - - - - - - - - - - -

- - - - - - - - - - - - - - - -

🏔️ My goal: What are you looking toward?

- - - - - - - - - - - - - - - -

- - - - - - - - - - - - - - - -

🎯 Today Targets: 30 Min. Time Blocks:

_____

- - - - - - - - - - - - - - - -

- - - - - - - - - - - - - - - -

_____

- - - - - - - - - - - - - - - -

_____

- - - - - - - - - - - - - - - -

🌟 What will make today great?

- - - - - - - - - - - - - - - -

- - - - - - - - - - - - - - - -

- - - - - - - - - - - - - - - -

Plan to reality score: _ _ _ _ _ _ /10

Progress towards goal

☐ last week   ☐ this week   ☐ remaining

"*dreams*
DONT WORK
UNLESS
you do"

（S）（M）（T）（W）（T）（F）（S）   /   /

⊛ Today I'm grateful for …

-       -

-       -

-       -

                                                    - -

⛰ My goal: What are you looking toward?

-       -

-       -

-       -

                                                    - -

◎ Today Targets: 30 Min. Time Blocks:

                                                    - -

_____   -

-       -

-       -

                                                    - -

_____   -

-       -

-       -

_____   -

-       -

-       -

☆ What will make today great?

-       -

-       -

-       Plan to reality score: _ _ _ _ _ _ _ /10

Progress towards goal

☐ last week ☐ this week ☐ remaining

"dreams DONT WORK UNLESS you do"

(S) (M) (T) (W) (T) (F) (S) / /

Today I'm grateful for ...

My goal: What are you looking toward?

Today Targets: 30 Min. Time Blocks:

What will make today great?

Progress towards goal

☐ last week ☐ this week ☐ remaining

"dreams DONT WORK UNLESS you do"

(S) (M) (T) (W) (T) (F) (S)   /   /

⭐ Today I'm grateful for ...

🏔️ My goal: What are you looking toward?

🎯 Today Targets: 30 Min. Time Blocks:

🌟 What will make today great?

Plan to reality score: _ _ _ _ _ _ _ /10

Progress towards goal

☐ last week   ☐ this week   ☐ remaining

"dreams DONT WORK UNLESS you do"

Ⓢ Ⓜ Ⓣ Ⓦ Ⓣ Ⓕ Ⓢ   /   /

⭐ Today I'm grateful for ...

- - - - - - - - - - - - - - - -   - - - - - - - - - - - - - - - -
- - - - - - - - - - - - - - - -   - - - - - - - - - - - - - - - -
- - - - - - - - - - - - - - - -   - - - - - - - - - - - - - - - -
                                          - - - - - - - - - - - - - - - -

🏔 My goal: What are you looking toward?

- - - - - - - - - - - - - - - -   - - - - - - - - - - - - - - - -
- - - - - - - - - - - - - - - -   - - - - - - - - - - - - - - - -
- - - - - - - - - - - - - - - -   - - - - - - - - - - - - - - - -
                                          - - - - - - - - - - - - - - - -

🎯 Today Targets: 30 Min. Time Blocks:

_____   - - - - - - - - - - - - - - - -
- - - - - - - - - - - - - - - -   - - - - - - - - - - - - - - - -
- - - - - - - - - - - - - - - -   - - - - - - - - - - - - - - - -
- - - - - - - - - - - - - - - -   - - - - - - - - - - - - - - - -

_____   - - - - - - - - - - - - - - - -
- - - - - - - - - - - - - - - -   - - - - - - - - - - - - - - - -
- - - - - - - - - - - - - - - -   - - - - - - - - - - - - - - - -

_____   - - - - - - - - - - - - - - - -
- - - - - - - - - - - - - - - -   - - - - - - - - - - - - - - - -
- - - - - - - - - - - - - - - -   - - - - - - - - - - - - - - - -

🌟 What will make today great?

- - - - - - - - - - - - - - - -   - - - - - - - - - - - - - - - -
- - - - - - - - - - - - - - - -   - - - - - - - - - - - - - - - -
- - - - - - - - - - - - - - - -   - - - - - - - - - - - - - - - -
- - - - - - - - - - - - - - - -   Plan to reality score:_ _ _ _ _ _ _ /10

Progress towards goal

☐ last week   ☐ this week   ☐ remaining

"dreams DON'T WORK UNLESS you do"

HABIT TRACKER ◯   MOOD: ☺ ☺ ☹ ☹ ☹   WIN THE DAY SCORE: / 10

Week Reflection

OUTCOME GOAL PROGRESS   % Completed ✓

	20	40	60	80	100
1.−	●	●	●	●	●

	20	40	60	80	100
2.−	●	●	●	●	●

	20	40	60	80	100
3.−	●	●	●	●	●

What worked and what don't

+   −

Moving forward, what things will you...

KEEP DOING

- -
- -
- -
- -
- -
- -
- -
- -
- -

IMPROVE ON

- -
- -
- -
- -
- -
- -
- -
- -
- -

START DOING

- -
- -
- -
- -
- -
- -
- -
- -
- -

STOP ON

- -
- -
- -
- -
- -
- -
- -
- -
- -

Who should thank / Ask for guidance moving forward:

- -
- -
- -

Weekly Planning

TOP 3 WEEKLY OBJECTIVES: Est. Time ☑

1.-

2.-

3.-

EVENTS & DEADLINES:

OTHER TASKS / ERRANDS:

"I don't have to prove anything to anyone. I only have to follow my heart and concentrate on what I want to say to the world. I run my world."

- BEYONCÉ -

WEEK 8								WEEKLY REVIEW
Day:								WK AVG
WIN THE DAY SCORE								
PLAN TO REALITY								
BUCKET LIST COMPLETED:								

WEEKLY REFLECTION:
Lessons learned, highs, lows, memorable moments, etc.

What did your key relationships look like this week?

How will I ensure next week is as good or better?

(S) (M) (T) (W) (T) (F) (S)   /   /

⭐ **Today I'm grateful for ...**

- -

- -

- -

- -

🏔 **My goal:**   What are you looking toward?

- -

- -

🎯 **Today Targets:**   30 Min. Time Blocks:

_____

- -

- -

_____

- -

- -

_____

- -

- -

✋⭐ **What will make today great?**

- -

- -

- -

Plan to reality score: _ _ _ _ _ _ _ _ /10

Progress towards goal

☐ last week ☐ this week ☐ remaining

"dreams DON'T WORK UNLESS you do"

HABIT TRACKER ○   MOOD: 😊 🙂 😐 😟 ☹️   WIN THE DAY SCORE: / 10

(S) (M) (T) (W) (T) (F) (S)   /   /

⭐ Today I'm grateful for ...

🏔 My goal: What are you looking toward?

🎯 Today Targets: 30 Min. Time Blocks:

✨ What will make today great?

Plan to reality score: _____ /10

Progress towards goal

☐ last week ☐ this week ☐ remaining

"dreams DON'T WORK UNLESS you do"

⭐ Today I'm grateful for ...

🏔 My goal: What are you looking toward?

🎯 Today Targets: 30 Min. Time Blocks:

🌟 What will make today great?

Plan to reality score: _ _ _ _ _ _ _ /10

Progress towards goal

☐ last week ☐ this week ☐ remaining

"*dreams* DONT WORK UNLESS *you do*"

HABIT TRACKER ○   MOOD: 😊 🙂 😐 😟 ☹️   WIN THE DAY SCORE: / 10

⭐ Today I'm grateful for ...

🏔 My goal: What are you looking toward?

🎯 Today Targets: 30 Min. Time Blocks:

⭐ What will make today great?

Plan to reality score: _ _ _ _ _ _ ./10

Progress towards goal

☐ last week   ☐ this week   ☐ remaining

"dreams DONT WORK UNLESS you do"

(S) (M) (T) (W) (T) (F) (S)   /   /

⭐ Today I'm grateful for ...

🏔 My goal: What are you looking toward?

🎯 Today Targets: 30 Min. Time Blocks:

✨ What will make today great?

Plan to reality score: _ _ _ _ _ _ /10

Progress towards goal

☐ last week ☐ this week ☐ remaining

"dreams DON'T WORK UNLESS you do"

HABIT TRACKER ◯   MOOD: 😊 🙂 😐 😟 ☹️   WIN THE DAY SCORE: / 10

⭐ Today I'm grateful for ...

🏔 My goal: What are you looking toward?

🎯 Today Targets: 30 Min. Time Blocks:

☆ What will make today great?

Plan to reality score: _ _ _ _ _ _ _ /10

Progress towards goal

☐ last week   ☐ this week   ☐ remaining

"dreams DONT WORK UNLESS you do"

(S) (M) (T) (W) (T) (F) (S) / /

⭐ Today I'm grateful for ...

🏔 My goal: What are you looking toward?

🎯 Today Targets: 30 Min. Time Blocks:

_____

_____

_____

🌟 What will make today great?

Plan to reality score: _ _ _ _ _ _ _ /10

Progress towards goal

☐ last week ☐ this week ☐ remaining

"dreams DONT WORK UNLESS you do"

Week Reflection

OUTCOME GOAL PROGRESS   % Completed ✓

1.—

| 20 | 40 | 60 | 80 | 100 |
| ● | ● | ● | ● | ● |

2.—

| 20 | 40 | 60 | 80 | 100 |
| ● | ● | ● | ● | ● |

3.—

| 20 | 40 | 60 | 80 | 100 |
| ● | ● | ● | ● | ● |

What worked and what don't

+   —

 Moving forward, what things will you...

KEEP DOING

IMPROVE ON

START DOING

STOP ON

Who should thank / Ask for guidance moving forward:

Weekly Planning

TOP 3 WEEKLY OBJECTIVES:

Est. Time ✓

1.—

2.—

3.—

EVENTS & DEADLINES:

OTHER TASKS / ERRANDS:

"I'd rather regret the risks that didn't work out than the chances I didn't take at all."
- SIMONE BILES -

WEEK 8								WEEKLY REVIEW
Day:								WK AVG
WIN THE DAY SCORE								
PLAN TO REALITY								
BUCKET LIST COMPLETED:								

WEEKLY REFLECTION:
Lessons learned, highs, lows, memorable moments, etc.

- -
- -
- -
- -
- -
- -
- -
- -
- -

What did your key relationships look like this week?

- -
- -
- -

How will I ensure next week is as good or better?

- -
- -
- -

Made in the USA
Las Vegas, NV
05 December 2023

82159738R00144